Essential Question
Where can your imagination take you?

A Fantastic Day!

by Clara Strongfoot

illustrated by Brian Dumm

Chapter 1
A Lake Made of Milk

Ramon sat in the kitchen. Mom gave him a glass of milk and two cookies.

Ramon thought, "The cookies look like two big eyes staring back at me!" Ramon had a great imagination.

Mom said, "I'm going to clean the living room now. Grandma is coming for dinner tonight."

"Okay, Mom," said Ramon. He stared at the big sponge on the sink. Ramon thought, "Wow! That sponge looks just like a cloud!"

Mom began to vacuum. Ramon thought, "That humming noise sounds just like an airplane!"

Ramon reached for a cookie. His hand knocked over the glass of milk. The milk spilled across his plate. That was when Ramon's imagination really <u>took over</u>!

milk

In Other Words took control. En español: *se encargo de todo.*

The spilled milk began to create a lake. The two cookies were islands in the middle of the lake. Two noisy airplanes flew overhead.

Ramon thought, "Wow! The airplanes are scooping up the cookie islands!"

Soon Ramon saw a fluffy cloud floating down to the lake. The lake started to shrink. Ramon thought, "The cloud is soaking up the lake!"

The lake and islands were gone. Then the cloud floated away.

Mom came back into the kitchen. She used a napkin to wipe a cookie crumb off Ramon's cheek. Then Mom said, "Let's clean up your room now, dear."

glass

plate

STOP AND CHECK

How has Ramon used his imagination so far?

Chapter 2

Getting the Job Done

"I know—it's a big mess!" Ramon said to his mom. They stood in the middle of his messy room. There were toys, blocks, clothes, and books all over the floor. Ramon's bed wasn't made.

Just <u>then</u>, the phone rang. "I'll see who that is, but you can start cleaning," Mom said.

Language Detective	<u>Then</u> is an adverb that tells when. Find another adverb that tells when on page 6.

Mom left, and Ramon's imagination took over again. He saw his toys come to life! Ramon thought, "My toys can help me clean!"

bookworm

Ramon's books inched over to the bookcase. Ramon thought, "Look at the bookworms! They are crawling to the right spot."

tornado

Seconds later, a tornado whirled through the open window. Ramon said, "Look at this thing spin and swirl!" It blew all the dirty clothes into the basket. It blew the sheets into place on the bed.

Mom looked in the room. It was clean and tidy. She said, "Good job! Grandma will be here soon. Let's go cook dinner."

STOP AND CHECK

How did Ramon's room really get clean and tidy?

Chapter 3

Sweet Dreams

At dinner, Ramon told Grandma about his fantastic day. He told her about the airplanes, islands, clouds, and lake.

Grandma laughed. "You have quite an imagination!"

Ramon told Grandma how his toys helped him clean his room. He wanted to tell her about the tornado, but it was time for bed.

Ramon put on his pajamas and got into bed. Grandma tucked him in and read him a story.

"Sleep tight, my dear," Grandma said.

Ramon said, "But I'm not sleepy, Grandma."

"You can count sheep," she suggested. Then she turned off the light and left the room.

In Other Words Good night. En español: *buenas noches.*

pillow

Ramon thought of sheep jumping over a fence. Then he stopped. "Sheep are boring. I could think of something more interesting," Ramon thought. Then his imagination took over again!

The moonlight became a dazzling ocean. Ramon saw dolphins leap through his bedroom window. He climbed onto the <u>largest</u> dolphin's back.

Ramon thought, "This is as much fun as an amusement park ride!"

window

dolphin

waves

Ramon rode with the dolphins to a sandy beach with rolling waves. "Whee! I'm a surfer!" he thought.

Soon, Ramon felt sleepy. "Even surfers have to nap," he mumbled. Ramon curled up on the beach. Soon he was fast asleep.

STOP AND CHECK

How did Ramon's imagination help him go to sleep?

15

Respond to Reading

Summarize

Use details to summarize *A Fantastic Day!*

Character	Clue	Point of View

Text Evidence

1. How do you know *A Fantastic Day!* is fiction? Genre

2. What is Ramon's point of view about the spilled milk? Include details. Point of View

3. What are the cookies compared to on page 5? Metaphors

4. Write about Ramon's point of view and his mother's point of view.

   Write About Reading

Compare Texts

Now read some poems about where your imagination can take you.

dog

door

Pablo and I

When Pablo and I go walking,
I do all the talking!
  And he listens well
To all the things I have to say!

We never, ever go too far,
Sometimes we don't even leave the yard!
  Unless my Mama
Says that it's okay!

Pablo may not talk a lot,
But he's the best friend I've got!
  He likes it
When I tell him what I know.

I love Pablo's hair, so black,
Wet nose in front and tail in back,
  That wags and wags
And says he loves me so.

My Tiny Friend

Suzy's in my pocket,
Suzy's in my ear,
Suzy is my tiny friend,
She's with me all the time.

Do you have a friend like Suzy,
That no one else can see?
My Suzy keeps me company,
She's with me all the time!

Make Connections

Where does Ramon's imagination take him? Essential Question

How do people in the poems use their imaginations like Ramon does? Text to Text

Focus on
Literary Elements

Dialogue Dialogue is the words that characters say to each other. Dialogue can help you understand a character's point of view.

What to Look for As you read a story, look for quotation marks, like these: " ". They show the words characters say to each other. Look at this example from the story.

"You can count sheep," she suggested.

Your Turn

Write a story that includes dialogue. Have your characters go on an adventure in their imaginations. Use quotation marks around the words each character says.